WORKBOOK

HOW TRUST WORKS

THE SCIENCE OF HOW RELATIONSHIPS ARE BUILT, BROKEN AND REPAIRED

A GUIDE TO PETER H. KIM'S BOOK

TENT READS

Copyright

Disclaimer

TABLE OF CONTENTS

ABOUT THE BOOK   4

ABOUT THE AUTHOR   5

INTRODUCTION   6

DISCOVER THE TECHNIQUES FOR CREATING, PRESERVING AND MENDING TRUST IN ALL FACETS OF LIFE.

CHAPTER 1   9

THE COMPLEXITIES AND SIGNIFICANCE OF FIRST TRUST

CHAPTER 2   18

THE CONSEQUENCES OF BROKEN TRUST

CHAPTER 3   28

THE PART APOLOGIES PLAY IN REBUILDING TRUST

CHAPTER 4   38

GROUP DYNAMICS: THE CONFLICT AND TRUST DOUBLE-EDGED SWORD

CHAPTER 5   48

REBUILDING TRUST: THE ARDUOUS PATH TO RECOVERY FROM PAST TRAUMAS

FINAL SUMMARY   58

ABOUT THE BOOK

How Trust Works (2023) explores the basic role that trust plays in building, breaking, and repairing relationships by delving into the complex mechanics of trust. It provides a thorough overview of how trust functions in interpersonal and social relationships and is supported by a wealth of research on trust restoration.

ABOUT THE AUTHOR

One of the top authorities on trust restoration in the world, Dr. Peter H. Kim, has spent more than 20 years investigating this area. He is renowned for his knowledgeable understanding of the mechanics of trust in interpersonal and social contexts.

INTRODUCTION

DISCOVER THE TECHNIQUES FOR CREATING, PRESERVING, AND MENDING TRUST IN ALL FACETS OF YOUR LIFE.

To what extent does trust play a role in your life? You'll probably say that it's not too bad. Our social fabric is based on trust, which allows us to pursue occupations, make friends, and conduct a wide range of other transactions—especially in the digital age we live in today. Even so, we frequently overestimate the credibility of others and find it difficult to defend our own when it is called into question. Unbelievably, there is a growing divide in how we perceive and handle trust in today's culture, which presents more difficulties in both social and personal circumstances.

In this guide, we will examine the complexities of trust, including how it develops, its weaknesses, and the crucial roles competence and integrity play in influencing how we perceive trust. You will learn about the difficulties in upholding trust and the long process of mending it, especially after transgressions. We will also learn about the psychological foundations of trust as well as useful coping mechanisms for navigating its shifting terrain in the social, professional, and personal domains.

CHAPTER 1

THE COMPLEXITIES AND SIGNIFICANCE OF FIRST TRUST

Ever wondered why you will meet someone for the first time and have this sense of trust towards them?, more like the benefit of a doubt. Defying the widespread misconception that trust must be acquired gradually over time. This phenomena casts doubt on the conventional wisdom that holds that people are essentially opportunistic, greedy, and selfish.

Fundamentally, trust is a psychological state in which one is prepared to tolerate vulnerability in the context of favourable expectations of other people. By distilling trust down to its essential elements—a psychological state, a readiness to be vulnerable, and a dependence on others' positive expectations—this definition captures the intricacy of trust. Although trust is frequently viewed in economic theory as a means of reducing risk, actual situations present a different picture.

People often trust others based on very little information, as evidenced by an experiment in which participants watched a job interview.

In a very short period of time, the participants showed a high degree of confidence in the job candidate they hardly knew, and they exhibited a good deal of trust in them. However, why?

This early trust is influenced by other factors. One important factor is the societal backdrop; laws, rules, and social conventions frequently influence trust. The degree to which a person is inclined to trust others is also influenced by their unique personality qualities. First perceptions and other quick cognitive clues influence our trust assessments. These assessments are an essential part of how we manage social interactions, despite the fact that they can be erroneous and give rise to biases.

High initial trust has many advantages. It makes society run better and encourages cooperation, which opens doors for new business possibilities and relationship formation. Fascinatingly, research indicates that people are more inclined to act cooperatively and morally when they are seen as trustworthy. This shows that initial trust can frequently lead to behaviours that validate that trust, making trust a self-fulfilling prophesy. But it can be difficult to keep this trust going. Although initial trust is essential to society's endeavours and plays a major role in the prosperity of nations, it is not impervious to be violated. To maintain confidence in society, it is essential to comprehend these transgressions and the strategies for handling them. Essentially, although while our innate tendency towards trust may come out as naive, it is also a necessary element of prosperous and successful social connections.

We'll look more closely at what transpires when this trust is violated in the following section.

Key Points:

1. Contrary to the belief that trust must be earned gradually, research suggests that people often exhibit a high level of trust right from the start.

2. Trust is a psychological state involving a readiness to tolerate vulnerability, dependent on favorable expectations of others.

3. Societal backdrop, laws, rules, and individual personality qualities significantly influence the level of trust people are inclined to demonstrate.

4. Initial high trust has advantages, fostering cooperation and societal well-being, but it can be challenging to maintain.

5. Trust, when violated, requires understanding transgressions and strategies for rebuilding it to uphold confidence in society.

Self-Reflection Questions:

1. How does societal backdrop, including laws and social conventions, influence individuals' initial trust in others?

_____

_____

_____

_____

_____

_____

2. In what ways can biases and quick cognitive clues impact our assessments of trust, and how can we mitigate potential errors in judgment?

_____

_____

_____

_____

_____

_____

_____

3. Reflect on a personal experience where you initially trusted someone quickly. What factors influenced your trust, and how did it evolve over time?

_____

_____

_____

_____

_____

_____

_____

CHAPTER 2

THE CONSEQUENCES OF BROKEN TRUST

When someone's trust is violated, the effects can extend far beyond the original transgression and impact all facets of the victim's life and relationships. Consider the tale of Ava. Ava was 27 when she was married to the man she thought would be her prince charming, but she quickly discovered herself in a violent nightmare. The way her spouse turned from a handsome suitor to an abusive partner rocked the foundations of trust, affecting not only Ava but also her kids, who saw their mother suffer. Her story illustrates the wider ramifications of a breach of trust in addition to the psychological suffering it causes, affecting not just herself and her children but also other people and societal structures.

As demonstrated by Ava's experience, betrayals of trust have long-lasting psychological effects. Deep emotional scars are left behind by these experiences, which overshadow the pleasant parts of relationships. Research has indicated that unfounded claims have the power to significantly erode trust, underscoring the brittle nature of confidence and our susceptibility to possible betrayals.

The idea of loss aversion clarifies why betrayals of trust have such a profound effect. Individuals frequently view losses—like betrayals of trust—as more important than comparable rewards. Because of this predisposition towards loss, trust transgressions have a more severe and long-lasting effect.

Learned associations might arise as a result of experiences of pain caused by breaches of trust. People become hypersensitive to comparable circumstances or stimuli going forward as a result. Physical objects can become triggers because of their association with traumatic occurrences; this is demonstrated by the fact that something as basic as an article of clothing linked to the incident can elicit tension and aversion long after the breach of trust.

Different perspectives on breaches of trust introduce additional complexity. Divergent opinions regarding the existence of a breach may arise from personal encounters and the quality of the partnership. The relationship's qualitative and quantitative components have a big impact on how trust infractions are viewed and dealt with. While violators might not realise the full depth of the harm done or could dispute the necessity and scope of corrective activities, victims might feel profoundly aggrieved and distrusted.

It is more difficult to rebuild trust than it is to gain original trust, extend forgiveness, or stop future transgressions. Understanding the intricacies of the transgression, such as elements of guilt, accountability, and the possibility of redemption, is necessary for trust restoration. It's not only about admitting wrongdoing; it's also about bringing conflicting ideas about the transgression and the offender's personality together.

Rebuilding trust is a complicated and difficult task. It entails appreciating the harm done as well as comprehending the various viewpoints and feelings expressed. For those affected by the ripple effects of broken trust as well as for the larger society at large, this is crucial for healing and moving ahead.

Key Points:

1. Betrayals of trust, exemplified by Ava's story, have enduring psychological effects that extend beyond the individual, impacting relationships and societal structures.

2. Loss aversion plays a significant role in the profound and long-lasting impact of trust transgressions, as losses are often perceived as more significant than comparable rewards.

3. Learned associations from trust breaches can lead to hypersensitivity to similar situations or stimuli, creating triggers that elicit tension and aversion.

4. Divergent perspectives on trust breaches arise from personal

encounters and the qualitative and quantitative aspects of the relationship, complicating the process of addressing and rebuilding trust.

5. Rebuilding trust is a complex task that involves understanding the intricacies of the transgression, acknowledging guilt, accountability, and the possibility of redemption.

Self-Reflection Questions:

1. How does loss aversion contribute to the profound impact of trust transgressions, and how can understanding this concept aid in addressing the effects of betrayal?

_____

_____

_____

_____

_____

_____

_____

2. Reflect on a personal experience where trust was breached. How did learned associations affect your reactions to similar situations or stimuli afterward?

_____

_____

_____

_____

_____

_____

_____

3. Consider a situation where perspectives on a trust breach differed between parties involved. How did the qualitative and quantitative aspects of the relationship contribute to these divergent viewpoints, and what challenges did it present in rebuilding trust?

_____

_____

_____

_____

_____

_____

_____

CHAPTER 3

THE PART APOLOGIES PLAY IN REBUILDING TRUST

One idea is essential to rebuilding trust: apologies. The divergent responses to apologies in various crisis scenarios serve as a powerful illustration of this. Consider the distinctions between the Johnson & Johnson-managed Tylenol disaster in 1982 and the 1998 Real Irish Republican Army bombing of Omagh. Even with the Real IRA's apology that included recognition of blame and regret, there was still suspicion and condemnation; nonetheless, Johnson & Johnson's proactive crisis management strategy was able to successfully rebuild public confidence.

In the realm of apology psychology, there are six essential elements. Expressing remorse is the first step. It is not only admitting that you did something wrong; it is also a deep emotional realisation of what you did and how it affected you. Offering an explanation, the second component, helps to reduce mistrust by providing crucial background information about why the offence happened.

Thirdly, taking ownership of one's part in the offence and going beyond simple admission are necessary for true responsibility acknowledgment. A proclamation of repentance, the fourth essential element, shows a real resolve to refraining from committing the offence again and denotes a shift in mindset or conduct.

The fifth component, offering to fix, is making concrete suggestions for mending the damage or restoring the betrayed confidence. Finally, although it's the least important step, humbly asking for forgiveness is nevertheless essential to humbly seeking forgiveness for one's sins.

These elements demonstrate that the efficacy of apologies lies not only in their expression but also in their content. The circumstances surrounding the infraction, including whether it concerns competence or integrity, also have a big impact on how well an apology works. In instances of competence violations, where the problem is more likely to be skill or knowledge deficits than moral failing, apologies are typically more successful. Apologies, on the other hand, are less helpful or even harmful when there are integrity infractions, which are frequently seen as deliberate.

An additional layer of complication is introduced by the legal concept of mens rea, or "guilty mind," which is based on the sense of intent. The purpose of a breach is a significant factor in how the apology is received and, in turn, in the process of rebuilding trust. This is especially difficult as intentionality is a highly individualised concept.

In general, the degree to which an apology is successful in restoring confidence depends on the specifics of the offence, the elements of the apology, and the perceived intention of the behaviour. Because of this complexity, apologising and their place in the delicate process of restoring trust—whether in interpersonal relationships, business crises, or social conflicts—need to be understood in a sophisticated way.

In light of this, let's examine how trust functions in group dynamics.

Key Points:

1. Apologies play a crucial role in rebuilding trust, as illustrated by the divergent responses to the Tylenol disaster and the Omagh bombing.

2. In apology psychology, six essential elements include expressing remorse, offering an explanation, taking ownership, proclaiming repentance, offering to fix, and humbly asking for forgiveness.

3. The effectiveness of apologies depends not only on expression but also on content, influenced by the nature of the infraction, whether competence or integrity-related.

4. Legal concepts like mens rea, or "guilty mind," add complexity, with the perceived intention of the behavior influencing the success of an apology in rebuilding trust.

5. Successful trust restoration through apologies requires a sophisticated understanding of the offense, apology elements, and the perceived intention behind the behavior.

Self-Reflection Questions:

1. Reflect on a situation where an apology was either successful or unsuccessful. How did the elements of the apology contribute to its effectiveness or lack thereof?

_____

_____

_____

_____

_____

_____

_____

2. Consider instances of competence and integrity violations. How might the nature of the infraction influence the reception and success of an apology in each case?

_____

_____

_____

_____

_____

_____

3. In your opinion, how does the legal concept of mens rea impact the acceptance of apologies in situations involving trust violations?

_____

_____

_____

_____

_____

_____

_____

CHAPTER 4

GROUP DYNAMICS: THE CONFLICT AND TRUST DOUBLE-EDGED SWORD

Various far-right organisations gathered in Charlottesville in August 2017 to demonstrate against the removal of a Confederate monument. This violent altercation with counter-protesters quickly spiralled out of control, highlighting the intricacies of group dynamics and their influence on conflict and trust in society. It brought to light the ingrained prejudices and group preferences that influence our thoughts and behaviours. This incident not only had devastating results, such as multiple fatalities and serious injuries, but it also served as a sobering reminder of the enormous difficulties in establishing and preserving trust between various societal sectors caused by such deeply ingrained differences.

An innate inclination to support one's own group gives rise to the phenomena known as in-group bias, which becomes more pronounced when perceived threats from out-groups materialise. In addition to promoting internal cohesiveness, this prejudice exacerbates disputes and makes the process of rebuilding trust more difficult, particularly when it comes to heterogeneous groups. It has been noted that trust is more easily established and maintained within a group than it is between groups, which results in different reactions and interpretations of trust breaches.

It's interesting to note that group dynamics can result in consensus-driven decisions that might not take into consideration outside perspectives. This is demonstrated in corporate environments where senior executives may agree on crisis management tactics without taking public opinion into account. Perceptions of trust violations are further influenced by power dynamics, as strong members of the outgroup are frequently thought to be more likely to intentionally violate trust.

Strong in-group interdependence can also have drawbacks, such as the breeding of corruption and immoral behaviour that is frequently interpreted by outsiders as representative of the entire group. This is demonstrated by the divergent responses to events like the deaths of Breonna Taylor and George Floyd, where the defences of police unions and public indignation clashed, exposing disparate perspectives based on group memberships.

The homogeneity ascribed to out-groups is a crucial factor that affects whether remedies are deemed suitable for breaches of trust. Accompanying this are observations of collective hypocrisy, as in the case of the reactions to the scandals at the University of Southern California, wherein internal ties resulted in varying reactions to comparable misbehaviour.

The threat of extremism and group polarisation is the last point to examine. This is especially true given the nature of social media, where like-minded people support and magnify extreme viewpoints. There is a remedy, though: being exposed to a range of group viewpoints helps promote more sophisticated and integrative thinking, which is necessary for resolving conflicts and reestablishing confidence.

In our increasingly divisive society, trust must be rebuilt through skillfully managing conflicts and navigating the complex web of group dynamics, prejudices, and perceptions. These circumstances highlight how important it is to value diversity and have honest conversations in order to promote a society that is more unified and understanding.

Key Points:

1. The violent clash in Charlottesville in 2017 showcased the complexities of group dynamics, ingrained prejudices, and the impact on conflict and trust in society.

2. In-group bias, influenced by perceived threats from out-groups, makes establishing and preserving trust between diverse societal sectors challenging.

3. Group dynamics can lead to consensus-driven decisions, sometimes neglecting outside perspectives, as seen in corporate environments and crisis management.

4. Power dynamics play a role in perceptions of trust violations, with strong outgroup members often perceived as more likely to intentionally breach trust.

5. The threat of extremism and group polarization, exacerbated by social media, emphasizes the importance of exposure to diverse viewpoints for resolving conflicts and rebuilding trust.

Self-Reflection Questions:

1. Reflect on a situation where in-group bias influenced decision-making. How did this bias impact trust dynamics within and between groups?

_____

_____

_____

_____

_____

_____

_____

2. Consider a case where power dynamics played a role in perceptions of trust violations. How did the strength or influence of certain group members affect trust perceptions?

_____

_____

_____

_____

_____

_____

3. In what ways have you personally experienced or observed the impact of group dynamics on trust, especially in situations involving diverse perspectives?

_____

_____

_____

_____

_____

_____

_____

CHAPTER 5

REBUILDING TRUST: THE ARDUOUS PATH TO RECOVERY FROM PAST TRAUMAS

There are cases where trust violations occur across generations. Societies struggle to mend deep-seated wounds and reestablish trust in the wake of horrifying tragedies like the genocide in Rwanda. These incidents are tragic not only for the immediate loss and suffering but also for the physical and psychological wounds that survivors still bear. The question arises: how can a society move beyond such profound breaches of trust?

This is where "transitional justice" comes in, offering means to address human rights violations beyond traditional courtroom settings. Recognising the crimes, appreciating their effects, and working towards healing and reconciliation are all parts of this process.

The Nuremberg trials, which centered on the sentencing of Nazi leaders, historically established a precedent for handling crimes against humanity. These cases demonstrated the shortcomings of conventional courtroom justice even if they were a major step towards achieving justice.

Their restricted focus meant that many cases went unanswered, and they were associated with "victim's justice," which may have been unfair and illegitimate.

Various strategies have been developed in response to these constraints. The Truth and Reconciliation Commission, or TRC, in South Africa symbolised a paradigm change in favour of restorative justice. It attempted to create healing via truth-telling and acknowledgment, allowing victims and perpetrators to relate their tales. While the TRC made achievements in healing the nation post-apartheid, it also received criticism for not fully addressing systemic concerns and failing to give total justice.

A different strategy was provided by Rwanda's Gacaca courts, which are a community-based legal system created to manage the large volume of cases pertaining to the genocide. These courts were successful in handling a high number of cases while also promoting some degree of communal reconciliation. However, they too were attacked for their one-sided nature and the failure to truly achieve justice and healing.

These transitional justice measures, while vital, are not without problems and critics. They often struggle to address structural concerns and may fail to offer comprehensive justice or heal societal divisions. Power dynamics can profoundly influence these processes, resulting in skewed narratives or incomplete reconciliation efforts.

The quest of truth is crucial to these reconciliation processes. Rebuilding trust requires both public acknowledgement of crimes and an understanding of their effects. But genuine peacemaking and trust-building in post-conflict countries are intricate, protracted processes that go beyond quick justice initiatives.

In the end, all facets of society must continue to dedicate themselves to the process of rapprochement and trust-building, even though transitional justice is crucial in correcting historical injustices.

Key Points:

1.   Trust   violations   across
generations, as seen in cases like the
Rwanda genocide, present profound
challenges for societies in rebuilding
trust.

2.   Transitional   justice,   beyond
traditional   courtroom   settings,
involves   recognizing   crimes,
understanding   their   effects,   and
working   towards   healing   and
reconciliation.

3. The Nuremberg trials established a
precedent but had limitations, leading
to the development of alternative
strategies   like   the   Truth   and
Reconciliation Commission (TRC) in

South Africa and Rwanda's Gacaca courts.

4. Transitional justice measures face criticisms for struggling to address structural concerns, providing incomplete justice, and being influenced by power dynamics.

5. The quest for truth is essential in reconciliation processes, but genuine peacemaking and trust-building are complex, long-term efforts that go beyond quick justice initiatives.

Self-Reflection Questions:

1. Reflect on a situation where you observed or experienced attempts at transitional justice. What challenges or successes did you notice in

addressing historical injustices and rebuilding trust?

_____

_____

_____

_____

_____

_____

2. Consider the limitations mentioned for strategies like the TRC and Gacaca courts. How might these approaches be improved to better address structural concerns and promote comprehensive justice?

_____

_____

_____

_____

_____

_____

_____

3. In what ways can individuals contribute to the process of rapprochement and trust-building in post-conflict societies, understanding that these efforts go beyond transitional justice initiatives?

_____

_____

_____

_____

_____

_____

_____

FINAL SUMMARY

In human interactions, trust is a crucial but delicate component that can be swiftly built and then readily lost. Broken trust has far-reaching effects on relationships and society dynamics in addition to personal experiences. Apologies are essential to rebuilding trust, albeit how successful they are will depend on the specifics of the infraction and the alleged motivation. Group dynamics, which are impacted by polarisation in society and in-group biases, make trust and conflict even more difficult. Lastly, the necessity of accepting different viewpoints and admitting the truth highlights the necessity of using transitional justice to confront historical atrocities in order to promote healing and the restoration of confidence in societies.

Printed in Great Britain
by Amazon

38530895R00036